Finding Tale

Third Grade
Talent
Show

Jeanie Stewart
Illustrated by Bridget Starr Taylor

Rigby®
A Harcourt Achieve Imprint

www.Rigby.com
1-800-531-5015

Tam could hardly wait to get outside with her jump rope when the bell rang for recess.

"Do you want to jump rope with me?" she asked her friend Yelena.

Yelena explained that she and Juan needed to practice for the third-grade talent show that night as she walked away.

"I don't want to hear about the dumb talent show," said Tam even though no one was close enough to hear.

A little dog on the other side of the fence barked and wagged his tail, but Tam didn't care.

Pierre and Frank noticed their friend standing alone, and walked over to the fence. "What's wrong, Tam?" Pierre asked.

"I don't want to be in the talent show because I don't have a talent," Tam said sadly.

"Everybody has a talent," said Pierre, "but you have to find it. We'll help you."

Pierre and Frank had decided to sing "The Star Spangled Banner" for the show, so they invited Tam to sing with them, if she knew the words.

Frank and Pierre put their hands over their hearts and sang, "Oh, say, can you see . . ."

Tam continued loudly, ". . . By the dawn's early light . . ."

The little dog on the other side of the fence lifted his head and joined in. Frank and Pierre suddenly stopped singing and put their hands over their ears. Then Tam stopped singing, followed by the little dog.

Pierre smiled and said, "Tam, you sing very loudly."

"My voice sounds like a police siren," laughed Tam.

Mon Yee came over to find out what everyone was laughing about.

"We're helping Tam figure out what her talent is, so she can be in the show tonight," Frank told Mon Yee.

"We just discovered that her talent isn't singing," said Pierre.

Tam looked down because she realized that she didn't have a talent.

"Everyone has a talent, and we'll just have to work a little harder to find yours," Mon Yee said as she tried to make her friend feel better.

Mon Yee pulled out a red ball, a blue ball, and a yellow ball. "My talent is juggling," she said as balls began flying into the air.

"Now, that's talent!" said Tam, wishing she was half as talented as her friend.

The little dog barked.

Mon Yee gave Tam a pair of balls and said, "Now just throw one ball up in the air and then catch it with the same hand."

Tam thought that it was easy.

Next Mon Yee wanted Tam to try using two balls. Tam threw the red ball with her left hand and the blue ball with her right hand, but she couldn't catch either one. The red ball went over Mon Yee's head, and the blue ball went over the fence and into the little dog's mouth.

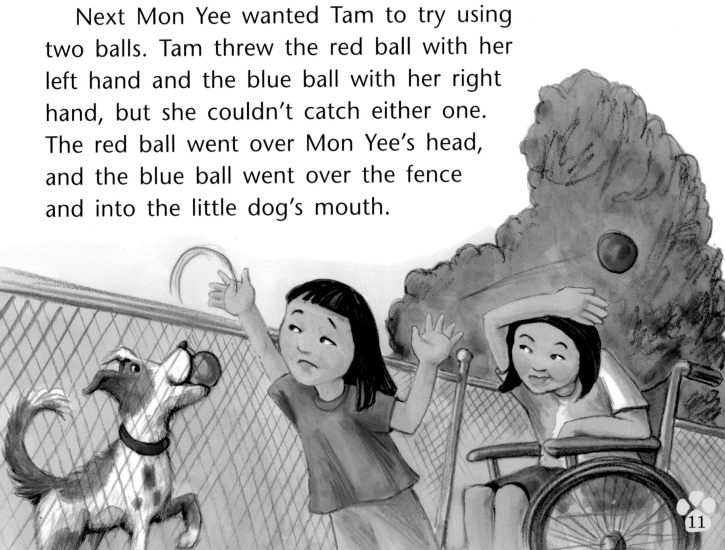

"Hey, little dog, Mon Yee needs that ball for the show tonight," said Tam as she reached through the fence.

The dog dropped the ball, and Tam grabbed it and went back to her friends.

"Well, juggling is not my talent either!" said Tam with certainty.

Claudine brought the red ball back to Mon Yee and asked what everyone was doing.

"We're trying to help Tam find her talent for the show tonight," said Pierre.

"Her talent isn't singing or juggling," said Frank. Everyone nodded in agreement.

Pierre said, "But everyone has a talent, and we promised to help you find yours."

"Maybe it's tap dancing," suggested Claudine, who took dance lessons after school.

As Claudine danced, her shoes made clicking sounds like snapping fingers. It wasn't hard for Tam to tap with her right foot. Then she tried tapping with her left foot.

Claudine took Tam's hand and said, "Dance with me, but now use both of your feet at the same time."

Tam tapped with her right foot, but when she tried to tap with her left foot, her feet got twisted together like a knot in a string.

Claudine was so busy tapping her own feet that she didn't see that Tam was having trouble. All of a sudden, Tam tripped and pulled Claudine down with her!

"Are you all right?" Tam asked Claudine.

Claudine said, "I'm fine, but I think that the little dog is laughing at us."

"Tap dancing really isn't my talent!" Tam said as she helped Claudine get up.

Claudine said that maybe Chang-Sun could help Tam.

"Chang-Sun, we're trying to find Tam's talent," said Claudine.

"I'll show her how to do a back bend," Chang-Sun said as he bent over until the top of his head was almost touching the ground. "Now it's your turn," he said as he stood up again.

Tam tried to bend over backward just as Chang-Sun had done, but she barely made it halfway over. No matter how hard she tried, she couldn't do it.

Just then the bell rang, and everyone but Tam went to the door. Tam walked slowly into school. She was unhappy because recess was over and she still had no ideas for the talent show.

"What's my talent?" she cried.

The little dog barked and wagged his tail, trying to get Tam's attention.

As she walked, she noticed that pieces of her uneaten lunch had fallen from her pocket onto the ground. "That must have happened when I tried to do that dumb back bend," she thought as she stuffed the leftover food back into her pocket. "I don't think I'm going to eat that for my afternoon snack," she laughed.

"I see that you have a new friend, Tam," Mr. Tran observed with a surprised look on his face.

"Oh, no!" Tam shouted when she saw the little dog standing behind her.

He explained that the dog belonged to Mrs. Escobar, the school principal. Mr. Tran offered to take the dog to Mrs. Escobar's office before the dog got into trouble. The dog hid behind Tam's legs when Mr. Tran tried to pick him up.

"Maybe if I walk to Mrs. Escobar's office he will follow me," suggested Tam.

"That's a good idea," said Mr. Tran.

Tam took a few steps and was followed by the dog.

"You are very good with animals, Tam," Mr. Tran said as he watched the dog follow quietly behind Tam.

"Maybe he knows that I have food in my pocket," she said as she smiled.

Mr. Tran told Tam to hurry back to class after she dropped off the dog because they were all going to practice for the talent show. He left her at the office and waved good-bye.

Tam wished that he hadn't made her think of the talent show again.

"There you are!" Mrs. Escobar said to the little dog as he followed Tam into the office. "Thank you for finding him, Tam. He followed me to school this morning and then ran off."

Mrs. Escobar patted the dog's head and said, "What am I going to do with you, Talent?"

The dog barked and wagged his tail.

Mrs. Escobar

"Did you just call him Talent?" asked Tam.

"Yes, isn't that a funny name for a dog? My daughter named him Talent because when he was a puppy, he could do so many tricks. But he only does his tricks for her," said Mrs. Escobar.

Tam laughed and said that every time she said the word *talent* today, he must have thought she was calling his name.

Talent barked and held out one of his paws.

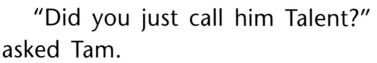

"He wants to shake your hand," said Mrs. Escobar.

Tam shook the dog's paw and said, "It's very nice to meet you, Talent."

Mrs. Escobar smiled and said, "I think he's happy to meet you, too."

"What other tricks does Talent do?" asked Tam.

"He can catch a ball, roll over, and stand up on his back legs," said Mrs. Escobar proudly.

"He sings, too!" added Tam.

"How do you know?" asked Mrs. Escobar.

"He was very loud at recess," laughed Tam.

Suddenly Tam had an idea, so she asked Mrs. Escobar if Talent could be in the talent show with her.

Mrs. Escobar said that she thought he would like that.

"Mr. Tran wants everyone to practice for the show, so may I take Talent with me right now?"

"Well, dogs don't belong in school, but I think it's OK just this one time," replied Mrs. Escobar.

Talent was quickly taken back to
Tam's class.

"Tam, can you show us what you are
doing in the talent show tonight?" asked
Mr. Tran.

Claudine put up her hand and said,
"Mr. Tran, Tam hasn't been able to figure
out what her talent is yet."

"But I *have* found my talent!" Tam said proudly.

Talent barked and wagged his tail, and Tam held out her arms and said, "I am Tam, the Animal Trainer, and this is Talent."

Mr. Tran shook Talent's paw and said, "Let's see what you can do."

Tam tapped her foot and invited Talent to dance. Talent jumped up on his back legs and danced. Mr. Tran and the class began to cheer because Tam had finally found her talent!